HERE COME
THE NUMBERS

ISBN: 978-0-9954750-7-6

First published in Great Britain in 2019, by Explaining Science Publishing.

HERE COME THE NUMBERS

by Kyle D Evans

Illustrated by Hana Ayoob

Here come the numbers,

All in a line.

They're good friends of yours

And they're good friends of mine.

Some round and tubby,

Some long and sleek,

But in their own way

They are all quite unique

Look at them all standing out on parade

These are the blocks

from which wonder is made.

3

But no matter how far or fast you might run

They never run out

– you can always add one!

Think of each one as a row of pink shells ...

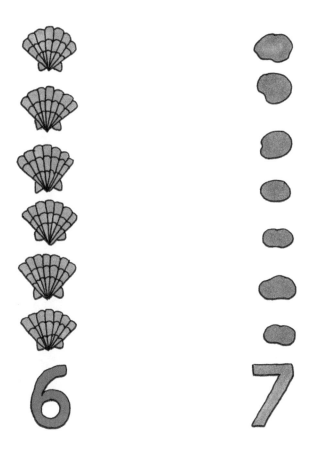

... or pebbles or buttons or whatever helps.

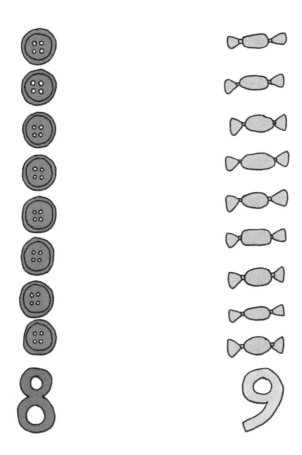

We can arrange them in
different shapes
And see all the beautiful
patterns they make.

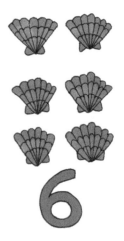

Some can form rectangles,
Some can form squares.
Some can't make either
– that doesn't seem fair!

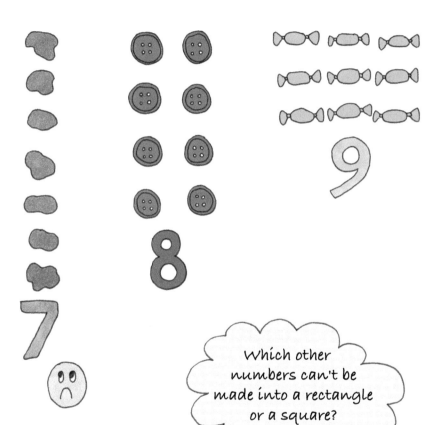

Which other numbers can't be made into a rectangle or a square?

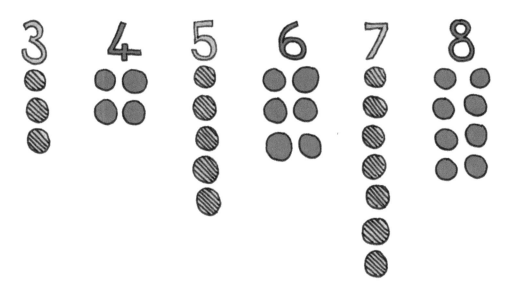

The awkward ones that have to stay in a line

Get their own special name:

We call them the 'primes'.

9

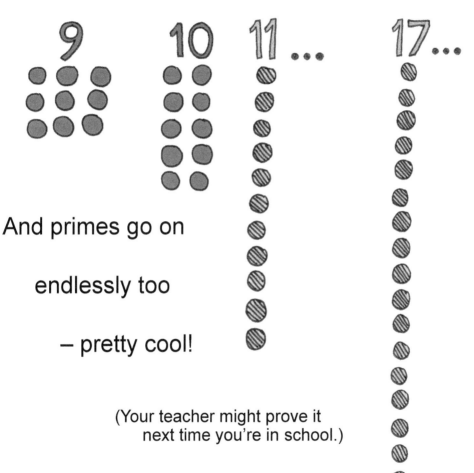

And primes go on

endlessly too

– pretty cool!

(Your teacher might prove it
next time you're in school.)

The odds are the ones

that won't go into pairs.

Put them together and

then you get squares!

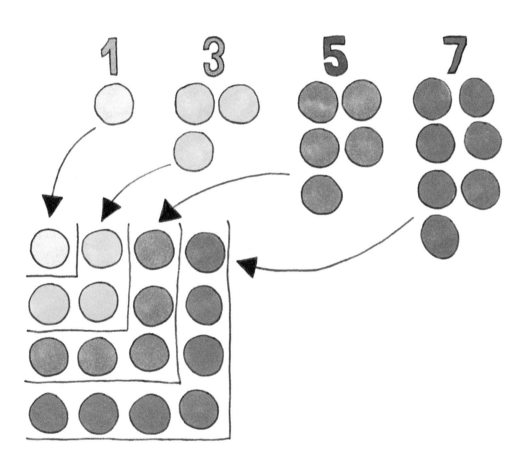

12

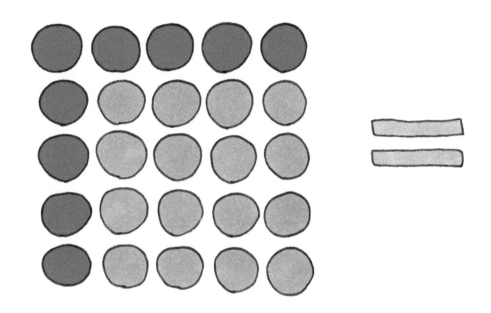

And while we're on squares,

Here's something way cooler:

Break up a square ...

13

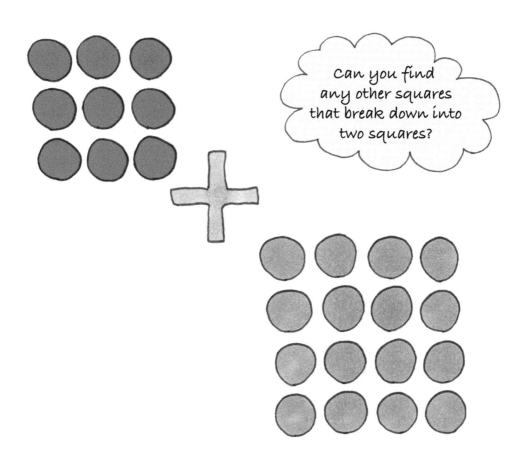

... into two that are smaller.

14

Though please don't try doing
the same thing with cubes.

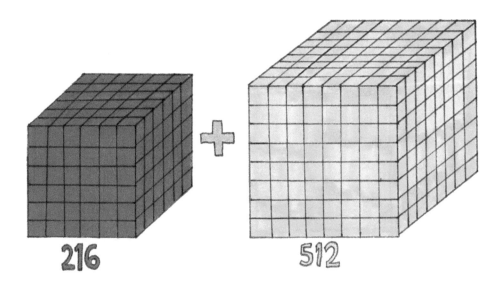

216

512

15

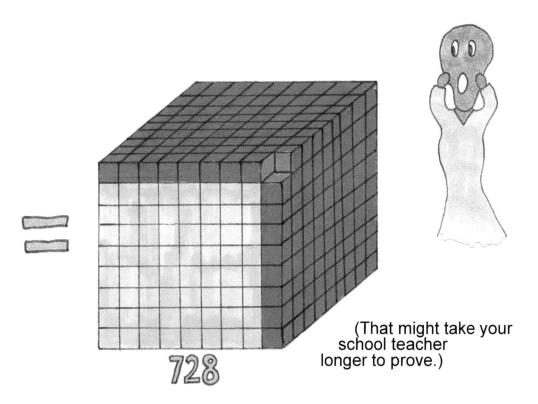

$\equiv$

728

(That might take your
school teacher
longer to prove.)

16

But that's not even half
of the numbers you thought. Look!
Over here's zero, a.k.a. 'nought'.

18

If you spent all the money you had in a year

– not one penny more –

you would find yourself here.

19

And
even though
it seems
incredibly
small,
it's really
the most
crucial
number
of all.

Raise all ten fingers,

then unclench your fists.

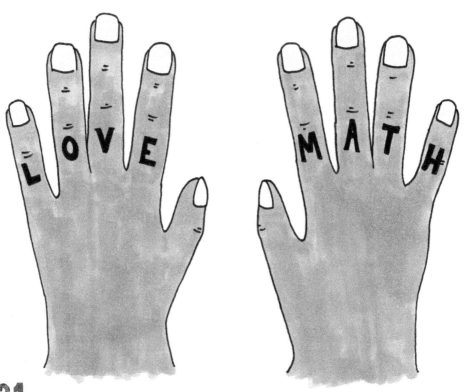

Without that fat zero ten wouldn't exist!

But who's over here? Hey, what a surprise!

The negative versions of all the same guys.

23

24

Though picturing these folks is tricky to do

... for 'minus two chimps'

isn't much of a zoo!

25

But if we can't see them, then
where can they be? Well ...

Say you had one pound but
went and spent three.

You'd find yourself owing
two pounds to the bank.

For that you have
negative numbers to thank!

28

And this is the most common

language on Earth.

Everyone knows what four dollars is worth.

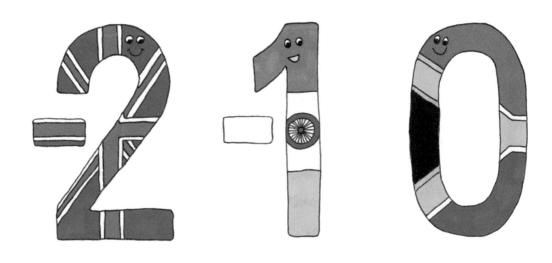

You might call it 'vier' but we surely agree:

it's 'ein' more than 'drei'.

(I mean 'one more than three'.)

ein   zwei   drei   vier

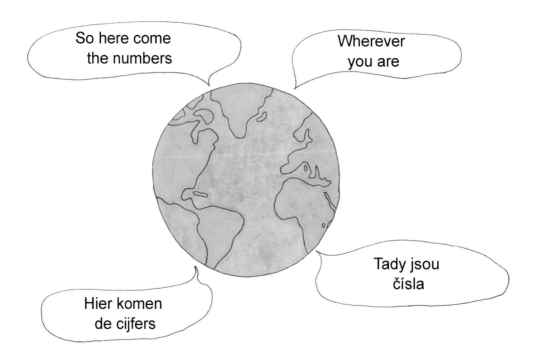

34

We'll see them tomorrow,

and every day.

Here come the numbers –

hip, hip, hooray!

Further notes for inquisitive folks......

Page 4: The number 1089 holds a special place in the hearts of maths enthusiasts – as you'll see if you check out the following trick, as a fun way of practising your basic addition and subtraction. Quick! Grab a pen and paper.

Pick any three-digit number (as long as it isn't the same forwards as backwards, like 121 or 333.) Now turn your three digit number backwards and subtract the smaller number from the larger. You'll now have a new three-digit number. (Take care if your first number has a zero at the end: reversing 240, for example, gives 042, and you must write it this way, not as the two-digit number 42.)

Turn the resulting number backwards and add the number you now have to the number you just had. Ta-dah! 1089! Here's an example starting from the number 123.

Reversing 123 makes 321.
Subtracting 123 from 321 leaves 198.
Reversing 198 makes 891.
Adding 891 to 198 gives 1089!

Can you work out why this will always work?

Page 9: Describing prime numbers as those that can't be arranged into a rectangle works almost perfectly – but note that 1 is not a prime number.

The fundamental theorem of arithmetic states that every number can be deconstructed in exactly one way into its prime factors, for example 12 = 2 x 2 x 3, and 90 = 2 x 3 x 3 x 5. If 1 was a prime number then there would be more than one way to write 12 as a product of primes, ie 12 = 2 x 2 x 3 x 1 = 2 x 2 x 3 x 1 x 1 and so on.

Proving that there are infinitely many primes is a beautiful example of 'proof by contradiction', or *reductio ad absurdum*, in which a statement is proved by assuming the opposite and showing that this leads to an absurd or nonsensical outcome. One way of doing it is as follows ...

First, assume that there are only three primes: 2, 3 and 5. Then consider multiplying these together and adding one. You would get 2 x 3 x 5 + 1 = 31. This number cannot be a multiple of 2, 3 or 5, since it is one bigger than a multiple of 2, 3 and 5. So it is either a new prime, or it can be made by multiplying two other primes we hadn't considered. Either way we have found at least one new prime, which contradicts our original assumption. This same process could be repeated with any length list of primes, to show that however many primes you think there are, there is always one more!

Page 11: This surprisingly neat result – that successive odd numbers add up to give square numbers – is thought to be the first published 'proof by induction', by Francesco Maurolycus in 1575.

Page 13: This page gives a visual example of Pythagoras' Theorem, possibly the most infamous rule in all of mathematics. I chose squares of sides length 3, 4 and 5, because 3 x 3 + 4 x 4 = 5 x 5 (9 + 16 = 25.)

But there are infinitely many Pythagorean triples, that is sets of side lengths that would work for my three squares. Some other neat examples are 5, 12, 13 (5 x 5 + 12 x 12 = 25 + 144 = 169 = 13x13), and 7, 24, 25 (7 x 7 + 24 x 24 = 49 + 576 = 625 = 25 x 25.)

Page 15: Even though there are an infinite number of uniquely different pairs of squares that could be put together to make another square, there are no two cubes that could be put together to make another cube.

Pages 15 and 16 give the closest example, missing by just one. Really: don't ask your teacher to prove this. It was first claimed to have been proven by Pierre de Fermat in 1637, but was first formally proved by Andrew Wiles in 1995 – some 358 years later!

Page 22: Counting systems without a symbol for zero, such as Roman numerals, have no system of place value and hence make even the most basic arithmetic very complicated.

The mathematician Fibonacci was instrumental in introducing the zero symbol to Europe in the early 13th century, but it was not commonly taken up for around another 400 years!

Page 23: For a long time negative solutions to problems were deemed to be 'wrong' or 'absurd'. Astonishingly, although negative numbers were used in China from around the time of Christ, they were not routinely used in Europe until a few hundred years ago.

You'll never be able to see a negative number of things, such as 'minus two chimps', but allowing negative numbers to be used means that we can do more maths than we could without – and who could argue with that?!

Kyle D Evans (www.kyledevans.com)
Kyle is a maths teacher by day, and award-winning
maths communicator and musical comedian by night.
This is his first book.

Hana Ayoob (www.hanaayoob.co.uk)
Hana is an illustrator, a science communicator and
a creative producer of science events.

Explaining Science Publishing collaborates with working scientists and science
writers as well as poets, artists and illustrators, to create books that aim to explain
scientific (and mathematical) ideas and inspire scientific thinking.

Want to know more? Check us out at www.explaining-science.co.uk